Flute / Oboe

TONS of TUNES

FOR THE BEGINNER

AMY ADAM
MIKE HANNICKEL

PLAYBACK+
Speed • Pitch • Balance • Loop

To access audio, visit:
www.halleonard.com/mylibrary

8010-7147-6557-5584

ISBN 978-90-431-1695-4

HAL•LEONARD®

Visit Hal Leonard Online at
www.halleonard.com

Contact us:
Hal Leonard
7777 West Bluemound Road
Milwaukee, WI 53213
Email: info@halleonard.com

In Europe, contact:
Hal Leonard Europe Limited
42 Wigmore Street
Marylebone, London, W1U 2RN
Email: info@halleonardeurope.com

In Australia, contact:
Hal Leonard Australia Pty. Ltd.
4 Lentara Court
Cheltenham, Victoria, 3192 Australia
Email: info@halleonard.com.au

Amy Adam, Mike Hannickel

TONS OF TUNES for the Beginner

Flute / Oboe

Audio arrangements by James L. Hosay

ISBN 978-90-431-1695-4

ARRANGERS

MIKE HANNICKEL grew up in the Sacramento, California area and attended California State University, Sacramento and the University of Southern California. He has been a music teacher in Rocklin, California since 1973. He also composes and publishes exclusively with Curnow Music Press with whom he has dozens of pieces of music in print.

AMY ADAM was raised in Grand Rapids, Minnesota and attended the University of Minnesota, Duluth graduating with a BM in band education and Flute performance. She has been a music teacher in California since 1992 and currently teaches in Rocklin, California.

TONS OF TUNES

TONS OF TUNES FOR THE BEGINNER is filled with the fun and familiar tunes that beginners love to play. All the songs have been arranged in keys that beginning band students learn in every popular band method. All **TONS OF TUNES FOR THE BEGINNER** books can be used together.

The **professional quality accompaniment recordings** can be used for practice and performance. You may also choose to purchase the separately available Piano accompaniment part.

The songs are in **carefully graded** order. You will find appropriate music for every level of early beginner.

TO THE TEACHER:

For private studio teachers: **TONS OF TUNES FOR THE BEGINNER** is an excellent and versatile choice for use in those early recitals. You can also encourage your students to put on concerts at home for friends and family using the included recordings.

For band directors: Motivate your students with these fun and easy songs! **TONS OF TUNES FOR THE BEGINNER** is designed so that any group of band instruments can play together. If, for instance, you have a beginning Flute, Alto Saxophone and Tuba player who would like to perform a piece together, you'll find what you need in this series.

Spotlight deserving young players in concert by including music featuring a soloist or small group. This also gives the band some needed rest.

TO THE MUSICIAN:

Have **FUN** playing these songs alone or with your friends! Even if you have different instruments, you can still play together. Each person needs to get the **TONS OF TUNES FOR THE BEGINNER** book for their instrument.

FOR THE BEGINNER

CONTENTS

PAGE

TONS OF TUNES
FOR THE BEGINNER

Amy Adam and
Mike Hannickel (ASCAP)

1. Mary Had a Little Lamb

2. Lightly Row

3. London Bridge

4. Twinkle Twinkle Little Star

5. Frere Jacques

6. The Party Song

7. Yankee Doodle

8. This Old Man

9. Aura Lee

10. The Snake Charmer Song

11. Bingo

12. Old MacDonald

13. When the Saints Go Marching In

14. Ode To Joy

15. Faith Of Our Fathers

11

16. Crusader's Hymn

17. Shoo Fly, Don't Bother Me

18. The Can Can

19. Mexican Hat Dance

20. Kum-Bah-Yah

14

21. Michael Row the Boat Ashore

Moderately (♩ = 108)

22. Oh Susannah

Moderately (♩ = 132)

23. For He's a Jolly Good Fellow

24. Polly Wolly Doodle

25. Pep Band Riff

26. Alouette

27. Skip To My Lou

28. I've Been Working On the Railroad

29. Here Comes the Bride

30. Amazing Grace

31. Grandfather's Clock

32. Take Me Out To the Ballgame